Non-Fiction Titles by Janvier T. Chando

ICONS AND VILLAINS: Recent Political Assassinations...
FALLEN HEROES: African Leaders Whose Assassinations...
UKRAINE: The Tug-of-War Between Russia and the West
Cameroon: The Haunted Heart of Africa

Fiction Titles by Janvier Chando

The Usurper: and Other Stories
Triple Agent, Double Cross
Disciples of Fortune
The Union Moujik
Flash of the Sun
Fortune Calls
Fortune's Master
The Girl on the Trail
Fortune's Children
The Norilsk Bears
Me Before Them
The Grandmothers and Perfect Love
The Fire and Ice Legend
The Sweetest Madness
The Hunger Fire
The Shades of Fire
Father and Sons
Fateful Ties
The Verdict of Hades
His Majesty's Trial
Ngoko's Folly
The Usurper
The Dowry
I am Hated
The Oaf

Upcoming Titles by Janvier Chando

The Home Drifters
The Mortal Friends
The White Hawk
The Norilsk Bears

Terror:
Political Weapon, Social Infection, Dehumaniser

Janvier T. Chando

TISI BOOKS

NEW YORK, RALEIGH, LONDON, AMSTERDAM

PUBLISHED BY TISI BOOKS
www.tisibooks.com

EPIGRAPH

"The time for revolutionaries with the complete freedom to maneuver is over."
            —*CHRISTOPHER NKWAYEP-CHANDO*

Acknowledgement

Dedicated to the loving memory of Christopher Nkwayep-Chando.

DEDICATION

My deepest, warmest, and everlasting thanks to Dr. Samuel F. Tchwenko and Christopher N. Chando for challenging me towards the path of humanity's enhancement.

Terror:
Political Weapon, Social Infection, Dehumaniser

Contents

Quotes

"Sometimes people hold a core belief that is very strong. When they are presented with evidence that works against that belief, the new evidence cannot be accepted. It would create a feeling that is extremely uncomfortable, called cognitive dissonance. And because it is so important to protect the core belief, they will rationalize, ignore and even deny anything that doesn't fit in with the core belief."
— **Frantz Fanon**

"Terrorists are not only those who believe they are chosen by God to commit mass murder in his name but can be governments and other systems of faith or worship that also believe it is their exclusive right to deprive others of their lives, freedom, prosperity, peace and harmony. When the majority in their communities, states or nations acquiesce to this twisted notion of exclusiveness, the people too get infected by the bug of terrorism and become dehumanized in the process without knowing it."
— **Janvier Tchouteu**

"Everyone's worried about stopping terrorism. Well, there's really an easy way: Stop participating in it."
— **Noam Chomsky**

"Let us not seek to satisfy our thirst for freedom by drinking from the cup of bitterness and hatred."
— **Martin Luther King Jr.**

"How can you have a war on terrorism when war itself is terrorism?"
— **Howard Zinn**

"Leaders who do not act dialogically, but insist on imposing their decisions, do not organize the people--they manipulate them. They do not liberate, nor are they liberated: they oppress."
— **Paulo Freire**

"Terrorism works better as a tactic for dictatorships, or for would-be dictators, than for revolutionaries."
— **Christopher Hitchens**

"Every empire, however, tells itself and the world that it is unlike all other empires, that its mission is not to plunder and control but to educate and liberate."
— **Edward W. Said**

"With guns you can kill terrorists, with education you can kill terrorism."
— **Malala Yousafzai**

"Most of the time, if you treat people right, you don't have to be afraid of them."
— **Kathy Kelly**

"I've never met anyone who wanted to be a terrorist. They are desperate people."
— **John Perkins**

"The difference between a terrorist and a freedom fighter is a matter of perspective: it all depends on the observer and the verdict of history."
— **Pentti Linkola,**

"The hallmark of an authoritarian idiot is yelling TERRORIST-LOVER! at anyone questioning the definition of Terrorist."
— Glenn Greenwald

"Stalin's Russia was a trap, in which even those running the system were caught. The leaders were trapped by fear of Stalin and even he was trapped by his fear of their desire to be rid of him. Everything he had to eat or drink had to be tasted by one of his colleagues first. Beria's behavior at his death showed that his fear was only partly paranoia."
— Jonathan Glover

"The greatest danger of a terrorist's bomb is in the explosion of stupidity that it provokes."
— Octave Mirbeau

INTRODUCTION

One story in particular in the bible intrigued me a lot as a ten-year-old trying to wrap his head around his Christian doctrine. That was the story of Samson the Hebrew or Israelite in the Book of Judges, whose divine-given strength enabled him to perform superhuman feats, including the slaying of a lion with his bare hands and the use of a donkey's jawbone in massacring a thousand Philistines. However, he tells Delilah, whom he is in love with, that the secret to his strength is his hair which has not been cut from birth. She passes this useful information over to the Philistines for money. After luring him to sleep, they cut his hair, and gouged his eyes; and then they put him to work in a millstone. The Philistines did not see it coming when they decided to celebrate Samson's capture in their venerated Temple of Dagon, and then brought and placed him by the main pillars of the crowded temple. Samson, whose hair had partly regrown, pulled down the pillars, killing the Philistines inside. He died in his act of revenge which was suicidal in every sense of the word.

Some pundits hold that it was an act of terrorism

because innocent women and children died from his action as targets he had in mind while executing his revenge.

Others hold that the civilians, including women and children who died in the temple, were collateral damages, as Samson's real target were the Philistine leaders who had assembled in the temple for the religious sacrifice to Dagon, a fertility deity highly venerated in the ancient lands of Mesopotamian Assyro-Babylonian (Iraq) and the Levantine (present-day Syria, Lebanon, Jordan, Israel, and the Palestinian territories), for Dagon's assistance in the capture of Samson.

Samson was a soldier all right, a man committed to the security and welling of the Israelites. However, heroic though his death was, it was an act of suicide. From the story of his conflict with the Philistines arises all the inner contradictions of war, especially armed conflicts where civilian casualties are unavoidable or are considered collateral damages or acts of terror. By Collateral damage, we mean deaths, injuries, or other forms of damage that those involved in an armed conflict inflict on an unintended target or property, especially civilians not involved in the war or that are not legitimate military targets. This is all the more disheartening because wars are supposed to be waged to free man from the tyranny of an oppressor. But then, what is the fine line?

Are attacks where civilian deaths are unavoidable

considered acts of terror?

This is where the line gets blurry for belligerents in an armed conflict— those trying to maintain the status quo as the authority legally responsible for the security of the people, and those who are confronting or are challenging the existing establishment (government, country, or organization) with arms. Civilians are always caught in their crossfire even though they are not supposed to be targeted. But then, what happens if civilians are targeted, whether in a limited or a broad manner?

This multi-million-dollar question has haunted humanity since time immemorial — whether from the mythologies of the Gods to our ancient civilizations, to the age of the assassins, to the times of Rome, and the spread of Islam, to the inquisition and on to liberation movements that created modern states. However, it is only in the last one hundred years that groups started waging wars where the principal targets are civilians. What makes these openly terrorist organizations somewhat intriguing is the fact that behind their strategy of using terror as a weapon, they have legitimate claims of persecution by the authorities they are challenging, claims that hardly anyone disagrees need redressing.

It is the room to maneuver or the range of actions within the disposal of those challenging the status quo that determines whether they have crossed the line into terrorism or not. And it is the response or actions of the government, state, organization, or group trying to maintain the status quo that also determines whether they are involved in state terrorism or not. How the world accepts or tolerates acts of terrorism differs in the eyes, hearts and minds of the different peoples, classes, and religions of this world. Those differences make taking a unified stance against terrorism all the more difficult.

This work is not an all-inclusive foray into the nature of terrorism or its history. Rather, it is a succinct account of the intricacy of terrorism, and its corrupting nature, especially for groups with legitimate causes that decide to embrace it. I mentioned examples, but the cases are not deeply illustrative. The idea is to pique the mind of the reader, to prod him to think deeper, analyze further and draw conclusions of his own that would only go to further the case against terrorism and help us all understand it better.

Chapter One

Terror or terrorism is the indiscriminate use of threats and violence for political purposes. It is perhaps the simplest strategy that a powerless or weak group or organization fighting an organized establishment is tempted to use. The nature of the organization of most terror groups, their support structures, and their objectives often constrain them, forcing them to operate:

- within a tight inner circle,
- with a great deal of fanaticism,
- with limited and thinly spread manpower,
- with light and limited materials or weapons,
- And with a clearly defined objective to bring down their opponents.

Perpetrators of terror with a clearly defined political objective are usually men who are highly committed to a cause but have little or no regard for the nature of its realization. These are people who stretch the notion of the phrase "Tragic Necessity" to the utmost, pitting their causes against humanity.

Terror is a powerful political weapon with a far-reaching social effect. And the recoil effect of an act of terrorism is unpredictable.

As a political weapon, terror might appear to be the most potent option by frustrated but committed advocates of a cause that has been sidelined, snubbed, and denigrated; or by a cause whose activities and members have been suppressed, repressed, and decimated by its opponents, the establishment, or the government. These advocates of terror often see themselves and their ideas as potential victims of annihilation at a time that they think they lack the means to openly resist. How far the organization embraces the methods of terror determines the degree of its dehumanization.

Terror fully embraced is more sinister, threatening, and sustainable if it has a base from which to recruit, train, regroup and replenish. The unacceptability of terror hinges the most on its social effects. And it can be very far-reaching indeed.

The use of violence and threats by a movement against a free, democratic, liberal, progressive, and humane society to intimidate or coerce it, always backfires, with the movement losing its humaneness and purpose in the process. Society in all its strata rejects the movement tainted by terror even if its cause promises to advance the wellbeing of the people. It was the case with the German group Baader-Meinhof, The Italian Red Brigade, The Japanese Red Army, and FARC-EP of Colombia today.

Even the Shining Path of Peru lost its purpose and folded because of the country's democratization and liberalization. And attacks by the Basque groups, ETA (Euzkadi ta Askatasuna), only go to denigrate the genuine grievances of the Basque people. The list is inexhaustible.

Acts of terror by a group or country against a foreign state, especially a free and democratic one, always have the opposite effect of uniting and mobilizing the state that is being terrorized. It makes the victimized state appreciate its humane values even more while enabling it to plug the loopholes that make it susceptible to acts of terrorism. The Irish Republican Army (IRA) actually got weakened in its fight against the British because of that. Palestinian Movements tainted their genuine cause with terrorist acts against Israel. Even the Separatist Chechen Movement is ruining its case with attacks against Russian civilians. The Lockerbie bombing and the 1994 Argentina bombing by suspected Iranian agents only strengthen the victimized countries. Above all, the country or group that accepts the use of terror even against the civilian population of the country they are against ultimately ends up dehumanizing its own society. That is because a policy of hate that justifies the killing of noncombatants, women and children always turns out to be xenophobic and full of lies; and it feeds on hypocrisy, brainwashing, ideological extremism, or religious fanaticism, which are all shortcomings that will ultimately lead to the demise of the propagators of terrorism and the breakdown of progressive human values in their societies.

With a base, terror suddenly unleashed against an unpopular, oppressive, repressive, discriminatory, detached, and elitist regime or government has an initial paralyzing effect on society in that it infuses fear, doubt and a sense of vulnerability into the minds of the oppressive class, while at the same time it stirs the common people into believing that the system they too are against could be brought down. The unleashed terror destroys the confidence the custodians of the repressive system had before, especially in their conviction that they could get away with all their actions against those opposing them. The members of the oligarchy suddenly become chaotic in their procedures, planning and execution of their strategies. The offensive nature of their rule becomes defensive all of a sudden without due preparation. The army and security forces, the administration, and the other agencies and organs enforcing the repression, oppression, fraud, corruption, discrimination, and violence become momentarily immobilized in the initial phases of terrorism.

With the terrorists striking at every possible target and with casualties rolling in, the custodians of the dictatorial system start questioning the justification of their policies, the prize they are willing to pay to stay in power and the chances they have of sustaining assaults from the terrorists. The foot soldiers of the regime (security agencies and intelligence services) that are the shields of the system or regime but not its benefactors, but who trace most of their origins from the majority of the people, start wondering why they have to bear the brunt of the anger against the system when they are not really responsible for it.

- Why would a patriotic corporal, inspector, captain, lieutenant, colonel, commissioner or general, or anyone for that matter who truly loves his country, wishes for its redemption and aspires for a better role in defending his nation, risk his life and the future of his loved ones by standing against the fire aimed at a corrupt, undemocratic, discriminatory and anti-people system and regime, while the leadership and its clique (the oligarchy) continue to swim in affluence and security?
- Why would these security forces risk their lives to maintain people in power who do not truly appreciate their worth?

The answer(s) to the above questions is simple. The defenders of the system would fight the terrorists to the bitter end only if they are convinced that the new order the terror organizations would bring with them would be far worse than the current reality.

Still, one cannot ignore the traumas in a society haunted by terror. Besides its infusion of fear and doubt into the establishment, and its destruction and immobilization of the tools of administration, terror as a political weapon used in a society that is not free, has the powerful effect of polarizing it. The unleashing of terror opens a conflict that:

- Pits the repressive oligarchy against the terror group, leaving the patriotic majority in the cold in their demands for democracy, freedom, and liberalism.
- Finds the have and have-nots drawn further apart.
- Widens the gap between the ignorant and the enlightened.
- Sets the docility of the old against the vibrancy of the young in their quest for freedom, democracy, progress, and transparency.
- Finally brings the idealists against the realists, the pragmatists, the humanitarianists and the dogmatists.

The use of terror in a genuine cause of freedom or liberation against the oppressive rule of an unrepresentative establishment becomes susceptible to blackmail, mistakes, and dehumanization. Even its limited use without a clearly defined direction exposes the majority of the soldiers and militants of the freedom or liberation struggle to the cruelest and most unusual of punishments from the oppressive system or establishment. The custodians of the system respond to the acts of terror with vile actions or remedies of their own that in effect constitute state terrorism. Inhuman in its content, the oppressive establishment nonetheless wins sympathy from the general population and the world at large. The regime suspends human rights; the regime goes further in its excuses and carries out preventive arrests, vile tortures, subornation, extensive legal murders (through questionable laws); and the regime executes cruel, vindictive, discriminatory and the most unusual punishments against those who oppose them, thereby bundling the terrorists together with the progressive forces of the land that are seeking liberty, freedom and/or liberation. Having lost the last elements of its humaneness, reacting out of proportion to the threat posed by the terrorists and the freedom demanded by the majority of the people, the oppressive regime, or the unrepresentative system in power presses on with open state terrorism through divide and rule by channeling its resources to stir deliberate violence and internal strife. In its desperation, the oligarchy strikes blindly and calculatingly in turns. Innocent citizens find themselves being hit more than the opponents of the system by both the establishment and the terror groups, with the terror groups finding themselves blamed for everything. This social chaos degenerates into civil strife with clans fighting against clans, tribes against tribes, religions against one another, races drifting apart, and the different classes becoming irreconcilable. In this situation where terrorism against the state loses its purpose, terrorism by the state prevails and saps the oppressed and freedom-loving majority of whatever little strength they might have left, forcing them to settle for any order the oligarchy can restore. In this case, the terror group's failure strengthens the dictatorship in power, enabling the system to last longer, even though it actually financed its state terrorism by using the public treasury and the sweat of the citizens.

A candid evaluation would, however, reveal that despite the possible glorification of terror by groups or people who feel cornered, the fact that the specter of mistakes or unfortunate accidents looms high takes away its effectiveness as a tool to realize the change that would enhance the wellbeing of the people. This is because these eternal questions vis-a-vis the use of terror need to be answered by any group that is using or planning to use it as a tactic or at worse a strategy:

- Where and who should the targets be?
- What is the purpose or objective?

A humane exponent of change who convinces himself that the use of terror is tragic but necessary in a tormenting situation risks corrupting his soul in the process, especially if his action gets out of control. Even the line that the use of terror should only seek to attract attention to the genuine cause of the unheard and neglected, is basically faulty because the use of terror often or always ends up as a boomerang. A genuine and popular cause tainted with terror that is ill-organized, poorly-targeted, and not clearly defined; one that that strikes at the establishment and results in civilian casualties as well, finds itself open to sabotage and blackmail, especially by leaving the door open for false flags.

The use of terror as a rule by genuine exponents of change is unacceptable. It subjects the movement to defeat, especially if it becomes a weapon of any duration. While a movement might be forgiven for using it as a spark, the shout that would immobilize the system and set off the avalanche, the effect of terror is corrosive against everyone and everything that it touches. And any duration in its utilization would blind the essence of the movement's true purpose, taking out the humanity embodied in struggles that involve the quest for freedom, liberation, democracy, prosperity, and human harmony; and as a consequence, it would open the ranks of the movement to blackmail and denigration. The most moral of men, the sanest of freedom movements, the most dedicated of revolutionaries and even humanists and humanitarianists of all stripes end up losing their purpose if they fail to consider the corrupting influence of terror, even in its short-term use, and especially when they fancy the use of terror as the rule or weapon of survival even against an inhuman establishment. By using terror, they end up betraying the hopes and aspirations of the struggling masses whose interest terror was first invoked to safeguard.

Short-lived Clearly targeted, purposeful, and organized terror in the activities of the ANC, SWAPO, ZANU-ZAPU and FRELIMO pushed the establishments in South Africa, Namibia, South Rhodesia (Zimbabwe) and Mozambique respectively to enter into the dialogue that brought the changes that enabled these liberation movements to win power democratically in those countries. The Islamic Salvation Front of Algeria lost its essence because of its blind adoption of terror. Communism considered by some pundits to be the most humane ideology in advocating for the economically and socially deprived people of this world lost its humaneness as a political force because of its initial embrace of terror. Lenin's short-term use of red terror during the Russian Civil War that followed the communist revolution was blown out of proportion when Stalin made it the rule of the Soviet system and a legacy that is haunting the communist ideology today. The examples of the fallouts from the use of terror are inexhaustible. That is why movements that are trying to advance humaneness should become self-critical when their leaders start flirting with the use of terror.

Chapter Two

In the case of Cameroon, the fact that the price for dislodging the system is high does not mean that effective use of terror against the establishment is the only option left. While it may appear attractive to some opponents of the Biya regime and the anachronistic French-imposed system as a whole, exponents of change should bear in mind the fact that even the most effective use of terror against the custodians of the system would likely denigrate the noble objectives of the century-old Kamerunian struggle and cloud the realization of the "NEW CAMEROON".

True an effective use of terror against those in the oligarchy with blood in their hands will mortify the system. True it would open a public debate and help to clearly identify the camps. And true it would indicate the seriousness of the forces advocating for a Cameroon with a sense of direction, in order to make it a country that has a place among the community of free, progressive, and civilized nations. But it would tear society apart and dehumanize it in the process, to an extent that its soul might even get more corrupted than it is at the moment. Mindful of the fact that some exponents of change who oppose the use of terror acknowledge the fact that its use would force the system to take the oppressed struggling masses seriously and make the establishment understand that their opponents can create a perpetual nightmare by making terror the rule in their struggle, exponents of change should never consider the use of terror in their quest to found the "New Cameroon" that is free, democratic, united, liberal, progressive, prosperous and pluralistic.

The UPC's (Union of the Populations of the Cameroons') war of reunification and independence for Cameroon, following its ban and suppression by the French Trusteeship authorities in 1955, is a classic case where a popular freedom or liberation movement's limited use of terror by retaliating against the French forces, and the forces of the puppet the French installed as president of Cameroon that were massacring the Cameroonian population, as well as those it considered traitors, was effectively turned around to give the movement a bad name as a bloodthirsty terrorist group. Through state terrorism, the UPC was denigrated, suppressed, and crushed and most of its leadership got killed, imprisoned, or exiled by the Franco-Ahidjo alliance. It was a campaign that went hand in hand with blackmailing and framing the movement, and at the same time stigmatizing the UPC's support base. It was so effective that the highly victimized Bamileké and Bassa peoples still find themselves the targets of stereotypes hatched by Jacques Foccart, the architect of French control in Africa, who did an effective job in presenting the UPC's war of freedom or liberation in the 1960s as a post-1960 ethnic revolt by the Bamileké and Bassa populations, thereby effectively casting the country's largest and most nationalistic ethnic group as a national enemy of the rest of Cameroonian peoples, a stigma that still haunts the country today. And men like Jean Forchive etc. owed their rise and prominence in the system to their successful use of state terrorism against the UPC.

There is a strong faction in the current Biya regime that envisages the eternal survival of the system through the careful use of state terrorism against the patriotic majority who are being allowed to use their voices, but not their hands and feet, in a sham process that allows for multi-party politics in Cameroon but that prevents democracy from taking roots by denying the people the right to choose through sham elections that make a mockery of democracy and freedom of choice.

In a nutshell, an organization that uses terror against an establishment, be it their home country or a foreign country, runs the risk of tainting itself forever, corrupting its essence, and plunging society into a process of dehumanization that may take decades and even generations to overcome.

Janvier Tchouteu   November 08, 1997

Glossary

Adamawa   The southernmost province that was carved out of the former Grand North Province. It is a plateau region.

Akonolinga   A town in the Center Region. It is also the capital of the Nyong and Nfomou Division.

Akum   A Ngemba settlement nine miles from Bamenda along the Bafoussam-Bamenda road. It is also a traditional Ngemba kingdom and the dialect of the people there.

Ambam	A town in the South Region. It is a sub-divisional capital in Ntem Division.
Ashia	Word used by both English and French-speaking Cameroonians to express sympathy, condolence, consolation, encouragement, compassion, harmony, understanding, agreement, thankfulness, and caution.
Bafang	The capital of the Upper Nkam Division and a Bamileké kingdom in the West Region.
Bafaw	The principal ethnic group in the area. It comprises the Kumba municipality. It is part of the larger Bantu group.
Bafedja	A settlement and Bamileké kingdom in the Nde or Banganté Division, West Region.
Bafoussam	The capital of the West Region and Mifi Division. Also, a traditional Bamileké kingdom.

Bafut	A settlement and traditional Ngemba kingdom about eighteen miles from Bamenda in the Northwest Region.
Bakweri	The principal ethnic group in the Fako Division, which is located in the Southwest Region. The Bakwerians are Bantu speaking of the Sawabantu subgroup.
Balengou	Bamileké settlement and kingdom in the Nde Division, West Region.
Bali	A Chamba settlement and kingdom about eighteen miles north of Bamenda, in the Northwest Region.
Bamena	Bamileké settlement and kingdom in the Nde Division, West Region.
Bambili	A settlement and Ngemba kingdom about nine miles north of Bamenda in the Northwest Region.
Bambui	A Ngemba settlement and kingdom about six miles north of Bamenda in the Northwest Region.
Bamenda	The capital of the Northwest Region

and Mezam Division.

Bamendjou	Bamileké settlement and kingdom in the Mifi Division, West Region.
Bami (Bamileké)	Diminutive of Bamileké.
Bamileké (Bami)	The most populous semi-Bantu ethnicity and the principal ethnic group in Cameroon. It is also the mother tongue of the people.
Bamilekéland	The western half of the West Region, with fringes in the Northwest and Southwest Regions. It comprises five administrative divisions, about ninety traditional kingdoms, and eleven dialectical groupings.
Bamoun	A semi-Bantu ethnicity and one of the principal ethnic groups in Cameroon. Also, their mother tongue.
Bamounland	The Eastern half of the Western province.
Bandekop	A Bamileké settlement and kingdom in Mifi Division, West Region.

Banganté	The largest Bamileké kingdom, the capital of the Nde Division, which is also its former name. Found in the West Region.
Bangou	A Bamileké settlement and kingdom in the Upper Nkam Division, West Region.
Bangoua	Bamileké settlement and kingdom in Nde Division, West Region.
Bangoulap	Bamileké settlement and kingdom in Nde Division, West Region.
Bantu	A Large group of Negroid peoples of Central, South, and East Africa that inhabits the forests of the Southwest, Littoral, Center, South, and East Regions of Cameroon. Also, the largest constituent of the Negroid or Black race.
Bassa	The principal ethnic group in the Littoral Region. It is Bantu speaking. Also found in the Center Region of Cameroon.

Batoufam

Bamileké kingdom in the Mifi Division, West Region.

Bawok   (Bahouok, Bahouoc)

Bamileké kingdoms speaking the Medumba dialect, found in the West and Northwest Regions. The principal ones are:

- Bawok-Banganté or Banganté-Bawok is a traditional Bamileké kingdom found in the Banganté subdivision, Nde Division. Much of the kingdom is in the city of Banganté. Following a series of strives in the early twentieth century, it lost most of its territory to the surrounding Bamileké kingdoms, with its subjects migrating to other areas in Cameroon and even founding new kingdoms.

- Bawok-Bali or Bali-Bawok: An offshoot of the mother

	kingdom of Bawok-Banganté, founded in 1907 with the help of the friendly Bali-Nyonga kingdom. It is an enclave in the Bali kingdom (*fondom* or traditional realm)
Bayangam	Bamileké settlement and kingdom in the Mifi Division, West Region.
Bazou	Bamileké kingdom in Nde Division, West Region.
Beti	Diminutive of Beti-Pahuin. It is also a subdivision of the Beti-Pahuin group of languages and is broken down further into Ewondo, Eton, Bane, Mbida-Mbane and Mvog-Nyenge.
Beti-Pahuin	Diminutive or shortened to Beti, this group of related peoples constitutes the third principal ethnic group in Cameroon. The ethnic homeland of the Beti-Pahuin people is in the Center and South Regions, with fringes and enclaves in the East Region. They are Bantu-speaking and comprise the following:

- Beti (Ewondo, Bane, Mbida-Mbane, Mvog-Nyenge, and Eton),
- Fang (Fang proper, Ntumu, Mvae, and Okak)
- Bulu (Bulu, Fong, Mvele, Zaman, Yebekanga, Yengono, Yembama, Yelinda, Yesum, and Yekebolo.)
- Smaller tribes or ethnic groups Pahuinised by the Beti-Pahuins such as the Baka, Bamvele, Manguissa, Yekaba, Evuzok, Batchanga (Tsinga), Omvang, Yetude peoples.

Beti-Pahuin people are also indigenous in Equatorial Guinea, Gabon, and The Republic of Congo.

Betiland   The Beti-Pahuin speaking regions of Cameroon (stretches from the southern half of the Center Region to the central and eastern parts of the South Region and extend as fringes into the Eastern province), Equatorial Guinea (Rio Muni), Gabon (the northern half), The Republic of

	Congo (the Northwest), and São Tomé and Príncipe.
Biafra	The short-lived Ibo-dominated state that seceded from Nigeria during the 1966–1970 Nigerian Civil War.
Bota	A suburb of Limbe, Fako Division, Southwest Region.
British Cameroons	The western third of the former German Kamerun that fell under British control following the partition of the German colony. It comprised British Northern Cameroons and British Southern Cameroons.
Boumnyebel	A Bassa village in Nyong and Kelle Division, Center Region.
British Northern Cameroons	The Northern half of British Cameroons that voted to unite with Nigeria in 1961, following the controversial United Nations plebiscite in the territory.
British Southern	The Southern half of British

Cameroons

Cameroons. Became part of the Cameroon Federation in 1961 following a plebiscite that resulted in its reunification with the former French Cameroun. It comprises the Northwest and Southwest Regions of Cameroon.

Buea

The capital town of the Southwest Region and former capital of German Kamerun.

Bulu

One of the peoples of the Beti-Fang ethnic group with a homeland in the South Region.

Cameroonian Pidgin

Also called Cameroonian Creole or Kamtok, it is the Pidgin English spoken in Cameron. It has five variants.

CDU (Cameroon Democratic Union). Called *UDC (Union Démocratique du Cameroun)* in French

A political party in Cameroon founded by Adamou Ndam Njoya, a former minister of the Ahmadou Ahidjo regime.

CENER

(*Center National des Etudes et de Recherché*)—Acronym of

Cameroon's secret intelligence service (National Center for Studies and Research)—that was changed in 1984 to *Direction Générale de la Recherché Extérieures* (DGRE)—General Directorate for External Research.

Center Region — The central region or province of Cameroon. Comprises eight divisions.

CNU (Cameroon National Union) calledin French UNC (*Union Nationale Camerounaise*) — Party formed in 1966 from the merger of the political parties operating in Cameroon. First Cameroonian president Ahmadou Ahidjo headed it.

CPDM (Cameroon People's Democratic Movement), called RDPC (*Rassemblement Démocratique du Peuple Camerounais*) in French — The CNU renamed in 1985. This is the party in Cameroon. Its former name (1966-1985) was the Cameroon National Union (UNC), which itself was formed in 1966 by the merger of political parties in Cameroon. Before that, it was called the UC (*Union Camerounaise*)---Cameroonian Union (CU), the former political party founded by Ahmadou

Ahidjo, the former President of the Republic of Cameroon. The CPDM/CNU/CU/UC has been the ruling party since the so-called 'independence of Cameroon in 1960. Paul Biya is the party's president.

CU (Cameroonian Union) called in French *UC (Union Camerounaise)*   Party formed by Ahmadou Ahidjo.

Douala   The largest city, economic capital, and capital of the Wouri Division and Littoral Region.

Duala   A Bantu-speaking people of the Sawabantu subgroup, they are the principal ethnic group of the Wouri Division and the Douala area.

East Cameroon   The French-speaking federal unit of Cameroon from 1961–72. It was formed from the former French Cameroun.

East Region   The Southeastern half of Cameroon. The East Region has four divisions with Bertoua as its capital.

Eton

One of the peoples of the Beti-Fang ethnic group. Found in the Center Region.

Ewondo

One of the peoples of the Beti-Fang group. Found in the Center Region of Cameroon.

Extreme North

A province in the far North of Cameroon. It comprises six divisions.

Free French Forces

These were French and Francophone fighters who continued fighting the axis powers of Germany, Italy, and Japan, even after France surrendered and signed an armistice agreement with Nazi Germany in June 1940. It was formed by General Charles De Gaulle, who was a member of the French cabinet on an official visit to Britain at the time of the surrender. General Charles De Gaulle strongly opposed French capitulation and the armistice signed by the new regime led by Marshall Petain that created the Vichy regime in the South of France, thereby allowing the North of the country to be under German occupation. He urged resistance against German control of France and its collaborationist Vichy puppets. The movement drew recruits mostly from the French empire, especially from French Central Africa, of which French Cameroun was the base at the time, under the new governorship of Jacques Philippe LeClerc. Philippe LeClerc led the Free French Forces' first major victory in the war with the capture in 1941 of Kufra, a town in the then Italian colony of Libya. It incorporated forces of the former Vichy regime in the colonies from 1943 and saw its ranks swollen by Frenchmen after the D-Day landing. The Free French Forces achieved their greatest glory with the liberation of Paris in August 1944, led by the French 2nd Armored Division because it had the least number of blacks in its ranks. By the end of the war, The Free French Movement constituted the fourth largest military force in Europe, fighting against the Axis powers. The right-wing political parties in France have been dominated by its members and the ideology of its founder called Gaullism.

FSD (Front Social-Démocrate). The SDF (Social Democratic Front) in French.

The political party that is described as the opposition leader in Cameroon. The SDF is led since its inception on May 26, 1990, by John Fru Ndi.

Fulfulde (Fula, Pulaar, Pular, Peul)

A Sene-Gambian language spoken by the Fulani people.

Fulani (Fulani, Fula, Fellata or Peul)

A mixed Negro-Tuareg people inhabiting the Savannah from Sudan to Sene-Gambia, they comprise three groups namely:

The Mbororo, Bororo, Burure or Abore who are pastoralists.

The Fulanin Gida, Ndoowi'en or Magida, who are fully sedentary communities.

The semi-sedentary Peul people who are agriculturalists and ultimately resume pastoralism, but often form permanent communities.

Foulanis, Fulanis or Peuls are the second most populous ethnic group in Cameroon. Found mostly in the northern provinces of Adamawa, North and Extreme North. Their language is the lingua franca of this part of Cameroon.

Foumban   The capital of the Noun Division and the Bamounland. Found in the West Region.

Foumbot   Agricultural settlement in the Noun Division.

French Cameroun   The Eastern two-thirds of the former German Kamerun that fell under the control of the French following the partition of the German colony by Britain and France. It became a French mandatory territory and later a trust territory from 1918 to 1960.

Garoua   The capital of the North Region and Benue Division.

Graffi — Pidgin German word for a grass field. A name often applied collectively to the semi-Bantu peoples of the Northwest and West Regions of Cameroon.

Graffiland — Cameroonian word for Western High Plateau, Western Highlands, or Bamenda Grassfields. Mountainous grassland region of the Northwest and West Regions of Cameroon. It comprises the Bamilekéland and Bamounland in the south, and the Ngembaland, Chambaland, and Tikarland in the north.

Ibo — One of the four principal ethnic groups of Nigeria. Found in the southeast.

Idenau — A town in Fako Division, Southwest Region.

Kamveu — The local council of notables among the different Bamileké kingdoms.

Koufra (Kufra) — An important but isolated Oasis settlement in the southeastern

Libyan desert that was of strategic importance for the North African campaign during the Second World War. Its capture from the Italians by the Free French Forces marked the first major battle won by France in the war, thereby boosting General Charles De Gaulle's prestige and the morale of the demoralized anti-Vichy forces.

Koutaba   A settlement in the Bamounland, Noun Division, West Region. Also, a major military and airbase in Cameroon,

Kumba   The largest city in the Southwest Region and capital of Meme Division. It is located about seventy miles north of Limbe.

KNDP (Cameroon National Democratic Party)   Nationalist party in British Cameroons. It led the campaign that realized the reunification of British Southern Cameroons with former French Cameroun.

Limbe   Former Victoria. It is the capital of the Fako Division in the Southwest

Region.

Littoral	The coastal province of Cameroon. It consists of four divisions.
Loum	An agricultural town in the Mungo Division, in the north of the Littoral Region.
Maguida (Magida)	Name erroneously used for the peoples of the Moslem North that originated from the third group of Fulanis—the Fulanin Gida, comprising the fully sedentary Fulani communities.
Mamfe	The capital of Manyu Division in the Southwest Region.
Manjibo	A Bamoun village in the Noun Division.
Mankon	Mankon is a Ngemba kingdom and part of the city of Bamenda.
Maroua	The capital of the Extreme North Region and Diamare Division.

Mayo Tsanaga	A division in the Extreme North Region of Cameroon.
Mayo Tsava	A division in the Extreme North Region of Cameroon.
Mbengwi	The capital of Momo Division in the Northwest Region.
Mboh	A Bantu-speaking people of the Mungo Division in the Littoral Region, with fringes of their homeland in the Southwest and Western provinces.
Mokolo	Capital of Mayo Tsanaga Division.
Molyko	A suburb of Buea in the Southwest Region.
Mora	The capital of Mayo Tsava Division.
Mutengene	A junction town to Limbe, Buea, and Tiko, in Fako Division, Southwest Region.
Nde	Formerly called Banganté Division. It is found in the West Region of Cameroon.

Ngaoundéré	Capital of the Vina Division and Adamawa Region.
Ngemba	The second most populous peoples of the semi-Bantu group. The Ngemba peoples are found in the northern half of the Cameroon Grassland (Western Highlands), mostly in the Mezam and Momo Divisions of the Northwest Region. The Ngemba people related dialects.
Ngembaland	The Southwestern part of the Northwest Region that is composed of several traditional kingdoms or fondoms speaking closely related dialects.
Nkongsamba	The capital of the Mungo Division of Cameroon. It is also the largest city in the area.
Nkwen	A traditional Ngemba kingdom and part of the city of Bamenda.
North Region	Central of the Grand North Regions. It comprises four divisions.

Northwest Region — A province from the former Federal unit of West Cameroon and the former territory of British Southern Cameroons. Peopled by semi-Bantu groups of Tikar, Ngemba and Chamba speakers. Their compatriots in the Southwest Region collectively call them 'Graffis'.

NUDP (National Union for Democracy and Progress). Called UNDP *(Union Nationale pour la Démocratie et le Progrès)* in French — A political party in Cameroon that was founded by Samuel Eboua, a former minister of the regime Ahmadou Ahidjo. Bello Bouba Maigari, a former prime minister of the Biya regime, usurped the leadership of the party and has been its president since 1992.

Nzui-Mantor — Banganté-Bamileké word for the panther or leopard.

OK (One Cameroon) — An offshoot of the UPC after it was also banned in British Cameroons.

Peul — A French term for Fulani borrowed from the Wolof language.

RDPC — The party in power in Cameroon.

*(Rassemblement Démocratique du Peuple Camerounais),*Called CPDM (CameroonPeople's Democratic Movement) in English	CNU renamed in 1985.
SDF (Social Democratic Front)or *FSD (Front Social-Démocrate)* in French	The political party that is described as the opposition leader in Cameroon. The SDF is led since its inception on May 26, 1990, by John Fru Ndi.
Semi-Bantu	The unique and unrelated peoples in Africa, comprising the Bamileké, Bamoun, Tikar, Ngemba and Chamba peoples.
Sokolo	A suburb in Limbe, Southwest Region.
South Region	Cameroon's southern coastal province. It comprises the three divisions of Ntem, Ocean and Dja and Lobo.

Southwest Region — Southwestern coastal province of Cameroon. It has four divisions. Formerly a part of British Southern Cameroons and the federal unit of West Cameroon.

Tcholliré — The capital of Rey Bouba Division in the North Region.

Tiko — A coastal town in Fako Division in the Southwest Region.

Tonga — Bamileké settlement and kingdom in the Nde Division, West Region.

Tuareg — A Berber-speaking people of the Mazigh group inhabiting the central Sahara from Southern Algeria and Tripolitania in Libya, to the middle Niger and the northern borders of Nigeria. They moved to the interior of the Sahara Desert to escape the Arab invasion of North Africa in the 7th and 8th centuries.

UDC (Union Démocratique du Cameroun) or CDU (Cameroon — A political party in Cameroon founded by Adamou Ndam Njoya, former minister of the Ahmadou Ahidjo regime.

Democratic Union) in English

*UNC (Union Nationale du Cameroun).*Called CNU (Cameroon National Union) in English — A political party formed in 1966 from the merger of political parties operating in Cameroon. It was headed by the first Cameroonian president Ahmadou Ahidjo.

UNDP (Union Nationale pour la Démocratie et le Progrès) or National Union for Democracy and Progress (NUDP) in English — A political party in Cameroon founded by Samuel Eboua, former minister of the regime Ahmadou Ahidjo. Bello Bouba Maigari, a former prime minister of the Biya regime, usurped the leadership of the party and has been its president since 1992.

UPC (Union of the Populations of the Cameroons) — First national and nationalistic party in Cameroon. The historic UPC was formed in 1948. Banned in 1955, it resorted to an armed struggle that continued well into the late 1960s.

Victoria — The former name of Limbe. Was founded in 1857 by British missionaries for the settlement of rescued or freed slaves.

West Region

The southern half of the Western Highlands of Cameroon. It is populated by the Bamileké and Bamoun peoples. It is also Cameroon's cultural and agricultural heartland and is remembered for its historic role as the center of the country's nationalism and liberation struggle against the French Army in the land. It comprises the six divisions of Bamboutous, Menoua, Mifi, Nde, Noun, and Upper Nkam.

Wolowose

Cameroonian word for a whore.

Wum

The capital of Menchum Division in the Northwest Region.

Yaoundé

Cameroon's second-largest city and national capital. Also, the capital of the Center Region and Nfoundi Division.

Maps

Global terror hot spots

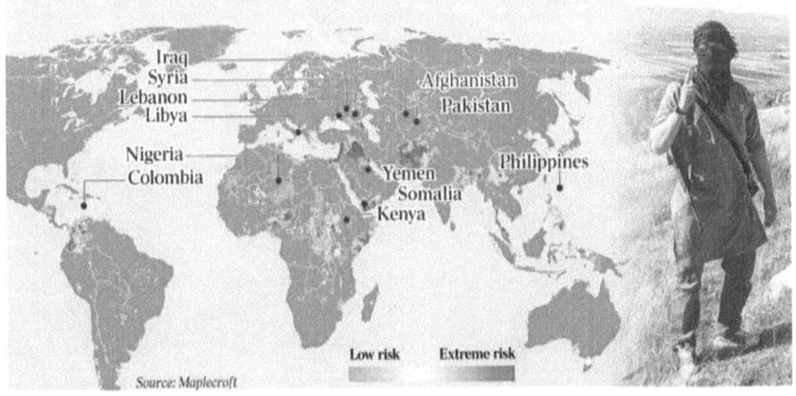

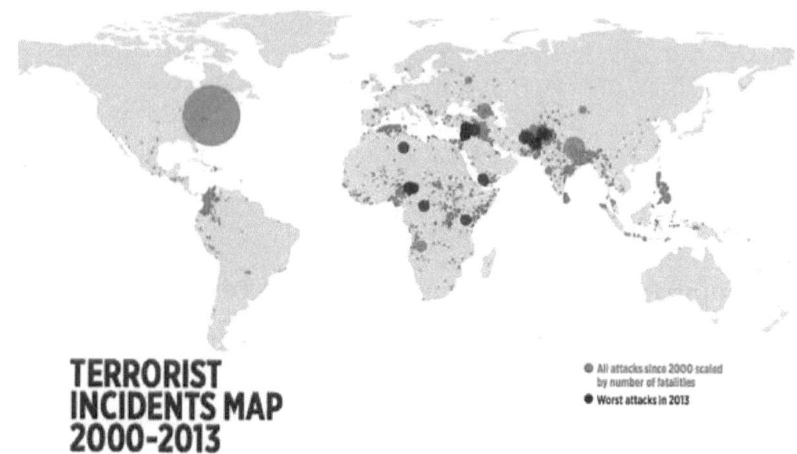
TERRORIST
INCIDENTS MAP
2000-2013
All attacks since 2000 scaled
by number of fatalities
Worst attacks in 2013

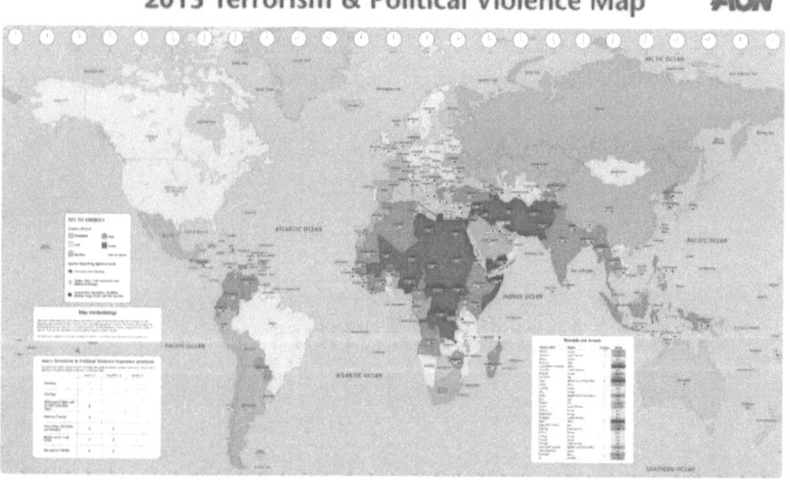
2013 Terrorism & Political Violence Map
AON

African Democracy Ratings

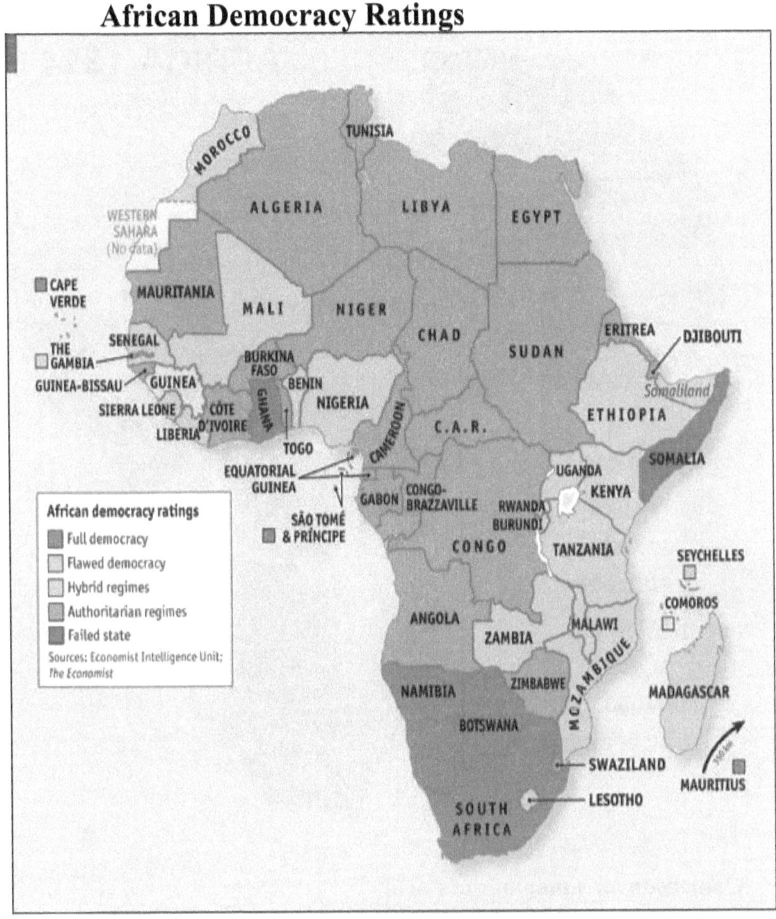

Partition Map of Africa: 1884-1914

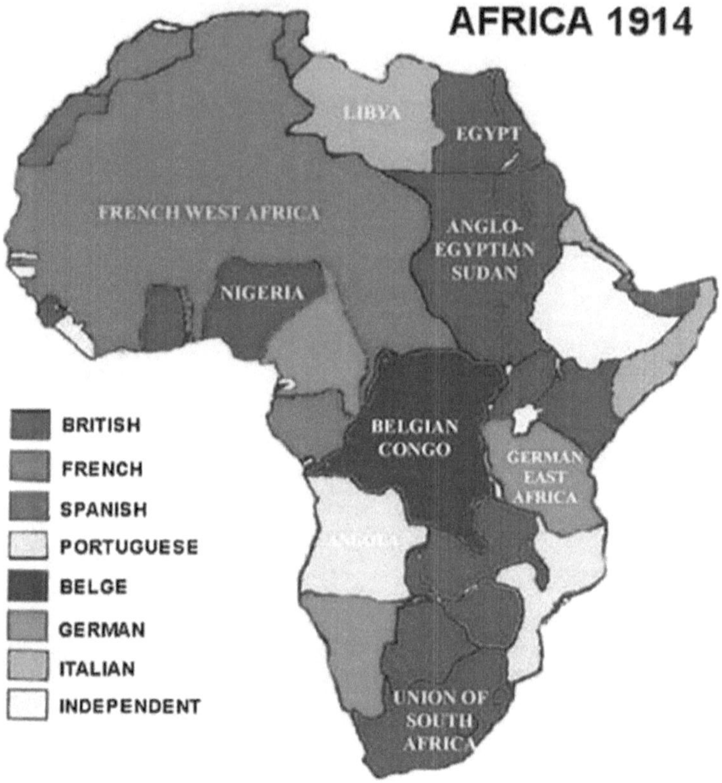

Cameroon on a map of the world

Cameroon over time

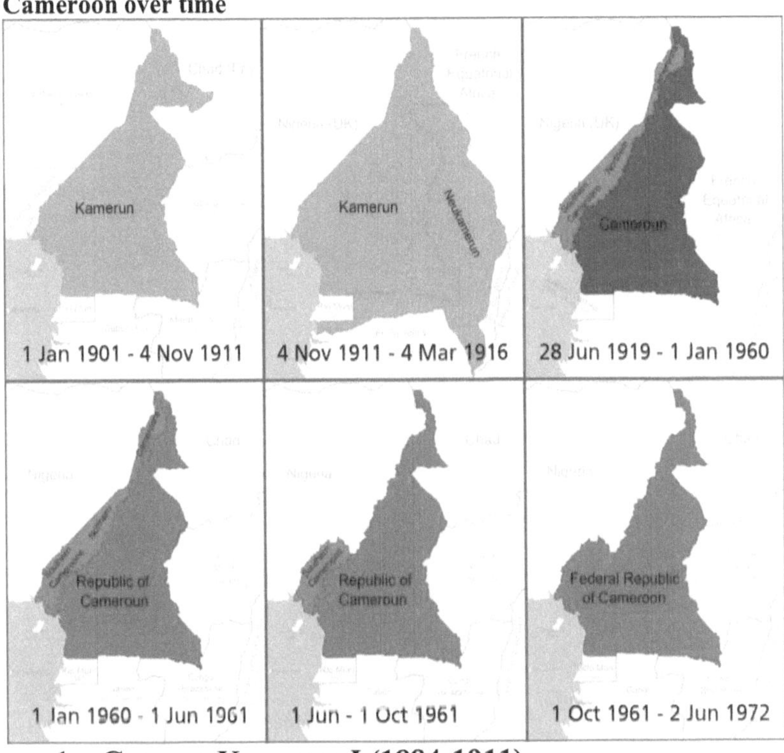

1. **German Kamerun I (1884-1911)**
2. **German Kamerun II (1911-1916)**
3. **British Cameroons&French Cameroun: 1916-1960**
4. **British Cameroons&La Republique du Cameroun (1960-1961)**
5. **British Southern Cameroons&La Republique du Cameroun (1960-1961)**
6. **Reunited/Independent Cameroon today.**

9 781981 013777